# BOOK SERIES
# REVIEWS FROM READERS

I recently downloaded a couple of books from this series to read over the weekend thinking I would read just one or two. However, I so loved the books that I read all the six books I had downloaded in one go and ended up downloading a few more today. Written by different authors, the books offer practical advice on how you can perform or achieve certain goals in life, which in this case is how to have a better life.

The information is simple to digest and learn from, and is incredibly useful. There are also resources listed at the end of the book that you can use to get more information.

*50 Things To Know To Have A Better Life: Self-Improvement Made Easy!*

Author Dannii Cohen

---

This book is very helpful and provides simple tips on how to improve your everyday life. I found it to be useful in improving my overall attitude.

*50 Things to Know For Your Mindfulness & Meditation Journey*
Author Nina Edmondso

---

Quick read with 50 short and easy tips for what to think about before starting to homeschool.

*50 Things to Know About Getting Started with Homeschool* by Author Amanda Walton

I really enjoyed the voice of the narrator, she speaks in a soothing tone. The book is a really great reminder of things we might have known we could do during stressful times, but forgot over the years.

Author Harmony Hawaii

---

There is so much waste in our society today. Everyone should be forced to read this book. I know I am passing it on to my family.

*50 Things to Know to Downsize Your Life: How To Downsize, Organize, And Get Back to Basics*

Author Lisa Rusczyk Ed. D.

---

Great book to get you motivated and understand why you may be losing motivation. Great for that person who wants to start getting healthy, or just for you when you need motivation while having an established workout routine.

*50 Things To Know To Stick With A Workout: Motivational Tips To Start The New You Today*

Author Sarah Hughes

# 50 THINGS TO KNOW ABOUT GOING BACK TO SCHOOL WHILE PARENTING

A Guide from a Graduate

Renee Jones

50 Things to Know About Going Back to School While Parenting Copyright © 2021 by CZYK Publishing LLC.

All Rights Reserved.

All rights reserved. No part of this book may be reproduced in any form or by any electronic or mechanical means including information storage and retrieval systems, without permission in writing from the author. The only exception is by a reviewer, who may quote short excerpts in a review.

The statements in this book are of the authors and may not be the views of CZYK Publishing or 50 Things to Know.

Cover designed by: Ivana Stamenkovic
Cover Image: https://pixabay.com/photos/work-life-balance-work-5333802/

CZYK Publishing Since 2011.

50 Things to Know

Lock Haven, PA
All rights reserved.
**ISBN:** 9798594567627

# 50 THINGS TO KNOW ABOUT GOING BACK TO SCHOOL WHILE PARENTING

## BOOK DESCRIPTION

Do you feel stuck in your current career? Have your career aspirations changed since becoming a parent? Are you wondering if you can juggle being a full- time parent and full-time student? If you answered yes to any of these questions then this book is for you...

50 Things to Know About Going Back to School by author, Renee Jones, offers an approach to finding academic success while raising children. Most books on returning to the classroom after having children tell you to wait until your children are older, or only when necessary for career advancement. Although there's nothing wrong with that, I've got another opinion. Based on knowledge from the world's leading experts and personal experience, I am here to tell you that you can in fact, be present for your ambitions and your parental obligations.

In these pages you'll discover helpful strategies that allowed me to successfully complete my second graduate program while raising four small children. This book will help you develop a necessary strategy in order to use your time purposefully, without giving up either one of your dreams.

By the time you finish this book, you will know the realities of dedicating yourself to continuing your education and your family. So grab YOUR copy today. You'll be glad you did.

## TABLE OF CONTENTS

50 Things to Know
Book Series
Reviews from Readers
BOOK DESCRIPTION
TABLE OF CONTENTS
DEDICATION
ABOUT THE AUTHOR
INTRODUCTION
1. There Will Never Be a Good Time
2. You Will Always Feel Guilty
3. You Will Miss Things
4. Know Your Why
5. Find a Program You're Passionate About
6. Be Creative With How You Use Your Time
7. Plan and Strategize
8. Give Something Up
9. Figure Out Your System
10. Build a Routine
11. Know When You Do Your Best Work
12. Schedule Everything That's Important To You
13. Say No When You Need To
14. Be Prepared to Defend of Defer
15. Do Not Apologize For Your Dreams
16. Let Yourself Down Last

17. Be Where Your Body Is
18. You Will Encounter a Curve Ball- Be Flexible
19. Be Honest About The Time Commitment
20. Apologize When You Need To
21. Know What Needs Extra Attention and What Doesn't
22. You Will Snap
23. Don't Sign Yourself Up For Extras
24. Save the Excuses
25. Act In Your Values
26. Complete Tasks in Chunks
27. Self-Care Will Look Different
28. You Will Be Exhausted
29. Find Support- You'll Need It
30. Look Ahead
31. Evaluate Your Routine
32. Surround Yourself with People Who Support You
33. Take Yourself and Your Goals Seriously
34. Do Not Wait For An Opportunity
35. Use Your PTO When You Need To
36. Set Mini-Milestones
37. Let Your Family See You Succeed
38. Treat Yourself
39. Intentionally Find Joy
40. Someone Will Get Sick
41. Give Yourself Family Due Dates

42. You Don't Know What You Don't Know
43. You Decide Your Timeline
44. You Might Change Your Mind
45. Mantras and Affirmations
46. Talk With Your Family Members
47. Select Your Non Negotiables
48. You Will Feel Overwhelmed
49. Just Show Up
50. You Can Do Hard Things
50 Things to Know

## DEDICATION

To the people who've never given up on me and encouraged each one of my dreams, Mom and Jim, you give me inspiration and strength to live each day with purpose. To our children, Maverick, Ace, Baerett and Aurora- you show me unconditional love, and challenge me to live in ways I never imagined. Each of you give me courage, allow me to fail, and show me what it means to live my true self. You will forever be my favorite people. To Tara Dunker, you inspired me to start writing- you gave me the permission I was too scared to give myself. Thank you for believing in me, and for encouraging me to share my authentic self with the world.

## ABOUT THE AUTHOR

Renee Jones, the author behind Three Princes and a Sweet Pea, is the devoted mother to four children under the age of eight. She completed her second master's degree in May of 2020, spending the first year of her Educational Leadership program battling a difficult pregnancy and the second with a newborn, one toddler, one preschooler and a first grader. Dedicating herself to furthering her education, while being fully committed to her family, she wrestled through the challenges of pursuing her dreams while being present for her family. Taking an untraditional route in the use of her degree, Renee currently spends her hours chasing her children, strengthening her marriage, working part time in the classroom and full time encouraging conversations through written advocacy in purposeful living.

Visit Renee's website for additional insight to living with purpose while raising children at, www.threeprincesandasweetpea.com

# INTRODUCTION

*"When it feels scary to jump,
that is exactly when you jump,
otherwise you end up staying in the
same place your whole life, and
that I can't do."*

Abel Morales

The sheer contemplation of taking action in moving yourself forward, is most likely, enough of an itch or reassurance that this, the act of actually enrolling in your next class, is exactly what you want for yourself. Going back to school can be scary, even without the monumental task of needing to keep children alive. Confronting the reality that, while not impossible, going back to school will be difficult. Here are a few, well fifty, of my best takeaways, as I sit on the other end of my most recent journey through continuing my schooling.

# 1. THERE WILL NEVER BE A GOOD TIME

There will always be a reason why going back to school while raising children is a bad idea. Your children will always need you; managing your time between your own schooling, your current career and being present for your family will always be a challenge. Do it anyway- sign up for the program, take the class and focus on one day and one check-list item at a time. Do not put your dreams on hold waiting for the perfect moment. Instead, create your moment, show up for yourself and get to work.

# 2. YOU WILL ALWAYS FEEL GUILTY

You are a parent, there never has been nor will there ever be a week that passes in which you do not feel guilty or contemplate how you could have better served your family. Guilt will surround you when you're sitting in class rather than your child's second grade soccer game. You won't always be the one to tuck your kids in bed, or lay with them while their fever spikes. Your mind will often wander off to details involving your own school projects, as you are supposed to be assisting your child with their homework. You will feel guilt; accept this very raw emotion and figure out a way to move forward. You are worth going after your dreams.

## 3. YOU WILL MISS THINGS

By making the choice to show up for your education, you are making the choice to miss events with your family. You will not have the capacity, even with the best routines and schedules to be present for everyone, everytime. You'll miss zoo trips, extended family birthday celebrations, and other minor milestones. Instead of focusing on the things that you will miss, become more intentional with the time you are sharing with your loved ones. If missing a Sunday night dinner is less significant than a Saturday afternoon soccer game, plan ahead and be present where you are wanted and needed the most.

During my graduate program, our class met in an untraditional setting. One Sunday a month for eight hours at a time, and then several weeks during the summers. The program was structured to serve it's student population: teachers. We were given our schedules a semester, sometimes even a year in advance. Inevitably, even though it was only one Sunday a month, I still managed to miss several bridal and baby showers for dear friends. Class, of course, was scheduled the morning after I stood next to a dear friend serving as a bridesmaid. I had little sleep, a complicated schedule, but I tried my best. Even with a lot of planning, I still had to miss important events. I felt heartache and guilt at times, yet I knew that focusing on my dreams was also critical for my own happiness, important enough to keep marching forward.

## 4. KNOW YOUR WHY

For me, completing the predetermined next step always seemed like a natural progression. Having more children, working towards the bigger at-home DIY project, or going towards my second master's degree. I always find myself working towards something, needing to be moving forward. I yearn for the challenge and the competition of what is next to come. Yet, what I've learned is the vital importance of evaluating why you want to consider your next move. Why do you want to go back to school?

Be careful in knowing your what (going back to school), isn't over shadowing your why (the purpose behind the work). Once you know why you are going to school, once you understand what motivates you, then you'll find the strength needed to push through on your hard days, and yes- there will be hard days. Find the why behind the what and post it somewhere- somewhere you'll see the reminder every single day.

For me, pursuing my passion to become a school administrator, the reasoning behind my enrollment in the Educational Leadership program, was to support students who were labeled as the "hard kid". Being the sibling to a person who struggled with ADHD and the labels and difficulties that came from adults misunderstanding or lacking the knowledge on how to handle or serve all kids. Turns out, my passions became even more personal, as I now serve as the mother, teacher and adult that not only my brother needed, but also that my own children need. My why, and understanding what motivates me helped push me forward, ask the hard questions and keep going during even the most difficult moments. You will not lose your motivation for your what, if you are constantly reminded of your why.

## 5. FIND A PROGRAM YOU'RE PASSIONATE ABOUT

Do the work for you, not a boss or spouse that thinks adding more school would be a great idea. Go back to school, not just for the pay increase, or to add one more plack on the wall, but because there is a fire lit inside of you. Find a subject you genuinely want to dive into for the next two to three years. Choose not only the degree that allows for your professional and personal advancement, but also the program that activates your development into becoming a better person. Strive to gain necessary legal certifications, and individual betterment.

## 6. BE CREATIVE WITH HOW YOU USE YOUR TIME

Most likely, adding the title of college student to your resume does not take away any of your current responsibilities. Adding assignments, time for classes and additional program requirements can feel impossible. Rather than becoming overwhelmed, get creative. Can you complete your homework alongside your children? Can you make a game out of getting your work finished? While completing my Educational Leadership Degree I often took my three older children to school with me on the weekends. I completed graduate work while they watched movies in my classroom, had office chair races in the hallway or played soccer in the gym. My boys loved being at Mom's school, and I used the extra weekend hours to complete necessary assignments.

## 7. PLAN AND STRATEGIZE

Make a monthly plan- write down family, career and education requirements. Start with non-negotiables, not just for school, but also events that are important to you and your family. Do not let due dates and deadlines dictate your weeks. Instead, utilize your extra time to get ahead, to better balance your workload- giving you wiggle room and grace should something unplanned pop up. And, as you know- with children, something often pops up.

With each large graduate assignment, I never penciled in the actual due date- you know, the one given by your professor. In my planner, the assignments turn in dates were written down a semester in advance, yet intentionally I placed the date one week prior to when the assignment actually had to be submitted. If the article summary and analysis was to be submitted by October 7, my planner marked it due on October 1. I always gave myself more time than I anticipated needing.

In practice, on Sunday evenings while planning out my week, and reflecting on each of the upcoming tasks, I would look ahead to see what assignments needed to be finished. I always worked on the next week's assignments a week before my scheduled due date. Therefore, I was always working on assignments at least two weeks in advance.

I needed the grace and flexibility of this system, because even the best laid plans fail- and fail often. An emergency staff meeting, doctor's appointment or sick kid frequently disrupted my beautifully planned week. Not having adequate time to finish assignments is stressful, giving myself wiggle room allowed me to be where I needed to be without pulling all nighters or becoming resentful about my chosen obligations.

Figure out a way to strategize how you'll use your time. Always schedule time to complete your assignments, read your papers, and edit each of your assignments. Take the time to plan for success- do not let your inability to manage your workload leave you stressed for time with your family or other obligations.

## 8. GIVE SOMETHING UP

I quickly figured out that I needed to show up for my family, career and school every single day. No one obligation was forgotten on any given day. I needed to think about, engage in and complete something for each of the three programs daily, or nearly every day. It became easily apparent that I needed to figure out what other things, in my life, I needed to give up. Adding in a morning workout, biweekly friend dinners, or award winning home cooked meals were not my current reality. I found a system to complete my non-negotiables, the things I wanted most, and everything else became less important. As in, forget about it until I walk across the graduation stage less important. I rarely watched tv and spent nearly all waking hours caring for my family, completing school work, or preparing lessons for my classroom.

Don't get me wrong, I did squeeze in time for date nights, craft projects with friends, and a few workouts. They just happened less frequently than when I was not in school. Find a way to do the items that are most important to you, and give up the rest- including the guilt that comes with forgoing some previous obligation. If you do not intentionally give something up, the universe will inevitably choose for you. Do not leave how you spend your days to chance-- be intentional about how you spend your time.

## 9. FIGURE OUT YOUR SYSTEM

When I was a child, I used to think the clowns at the Shrine Circus were incredibly impressive. They'd walk between each of the three stages, all while juggling bowling pins, balls or even rings of fire. I'd look over at my mom, incredibly impressed by this yearly wonder. Ironically, I had no idea, as a single-mother of two children, one of special needs, that she herself was far more impressive than these clowns. She was literally juggling all three of our lives, and seemingly with ease.

For me, the best system I created was a simple two to-do list structure. In one motivational quote journal, I'd keep a weekly running to-do list. A sort of brain dump of all of the things I needed to complete in the next seven days. Work, home, school- everything went on the same list. Every morning, revisiting my large to-do list, I'd evaluate the top three things that needed my attention. I'd then put those three things on a separate sticky note, placing the sticky note at the bottom right corner of my keyboard. Each time I sat down to do something, I'd see my 'must do today' items. Once those were complete, I'd move to my endless constantly evolving list. This system was simple, and yet- very effective. And much like planning for everything, I wrote down everything- I gave myself credit for completing every task.

Figure out a system that works for you, then use it voraciously.

## 10. BUILD A ROUTINE

Stop scrambling to get things done and build a routine that sets you up for success. For me, waking up at 4:30 am, before the 6am internal alarm clock that our children have, allows me time to prepare for the day, a way to to mentally get ready to do all the things. I take time to listen to audible books or uplifting podcasts, curl my hair, cook breakfast, pack lunches or fold laundry. Waking up early provides me mental space to wake up and take care of myself, before I help take care of the seemingly endless tasks that it takes for our four small children to be ready for the day.

During the school year, as a teacher, the seventh and final hour bell rang at 3:00pm. I often allowed myself fifteen minutes to decompress, take a small walk to make copies, refill my water bottle, whatever it is that I needed that day. Yet, promptly at 3:15, with intention, it was classroom door closed, head down and work like it's game seven. Every. Single. Day. I had until 4:45pm, a power ninety minutes to finish grading, lesson plan, call for doctor's appointments, schedule items and write graduate assignments. I always had a plan, and a list of the top three things that needed to be accomplished during that time. This time was both exhilarating, and exhausting. Using this time purposefully allowed me to eat dinner with my family, read bedtime stories with our children and get to sleep at a reasonable hour.

# 11. KNOW WHEN YOU DO YOUR BEST WORK

Finding extra time, in an already very busy schedule seems like an unlikely task. However, when something is important to you, you'll always find the time. Act smart, and be realistic with yourself. Do not sign yourself up for a late night study session, if your brain doesn't function well after 8:00pm. If you work better in the morning, move your alarm up an hour or so and get things done then. Use your strengths to move you forward, purposefully giving yourself the largest advantage in tackling your to-do list.

I often joke with my family that my brain just shuts down after 7:30pm. By 8:00pm, my patience starts to tire and all bets are off for consistent self-regulation once the clock ticks past 8:29pm. If by 8:30pm I am not lounging in bed or doing anything besides decompressing, then I simply become hard to live with or be around. Being productive during the late evening hours does not equate to productivity for me. Accepting when I am at my best and working my schedule around my strengths have allowed me to accomplish much more in less time.

# 12. SCHEDULE EVERYTHING THAT'S IMPORTANT TO YOU

Keep yourself accountable by keeping an inventory of everything that is important to you. If you don't have a literal list of important people and tasks, then get going- I am advocating for you to literally put pencil to paper. There is a way to complete all of the things that are essential to you, but you first have to figure out what those things are. Examples may include: one-on-one time with each of your children, a dinner birthday with your spouse, a reflection on a twenty-page article, a walk with your mother. If the task, big or small, is important to you, make a plan and a time to complete them. Be realistic with your time, understanding that while it may, on paper, seem reasonable to be booked solid for fourteen hours a day, five days a week, you will likely burn out. If needed, prioritize the inventory that you took about the tasks and individuals you value the most. Take the time to plan things out, it will almost always save you time in the long run.

## 13. SAY NO WHEN YOU NEED TO

Stop signing yourself up for unnecessary tasks. Chasing your dreams and attempting to please everyone at the same time will not be a realistic way to live. You will not have the time, or energy to be the class mom, prepare home made Valentine's cookies, or sign up for an extra job shadow. Saying no does not provide you with less worth, it simply means that you are saying yes to the responsibilities that are most important to you. Say no to the things that sound stressful, do not bring you joy, or are not a requirement from your family, your job or your schooling. You have enough to do- do not sign yourself up for more than you need to accomplish.

## 14. BE PREPARED TO DEFEND OF DEFER

Likely without attempts to be rude, people, sometimes, yes- even people you love, will ask you why you'd choose to go back to school rather than dedicate yourself wholly to your family. Defend or defer if you need to, but stand strong enough in your decision that you understand why this journey is important to you. Do not let other people's judgement influence your desire to pursue your passions.

## 15. DO NOT APOLOGIZE FOR YOUR DREAMS

As an individual, you alone are deserving of reaching for your dreams. You are worthy of furthering your education, chasing your passions and growing as an individual. Do not apologize for having class, needing to complete an assignment or putting in the work to accomplish this achievement. Do not use your dream as an excuse to treat people unfairly, or to miss events that are important to you, but also do not apologize that you are choosing to make yourself a priority.

Several times during my graduate courses, especially when I was visibly pregnant or when people knew I had a newborn baby at home, they would share their concern regarding my commitment to my family. The on looker was either commending me for being superwoman, or provided passive aggressive commentary about my decision not to, in their eyes, be putting my family first. Well intended or not, these comments became, at times, difficult to digest and sometimes hard to handle.

These opinions, while not far from the internal dialogue I had with myself from time to time, were not helpful. Not one time did I walk away from these conversations feeling better. Instead, after deep reflection, I committed to revamping my thinking, and simply stopped apologizing for my dreams. As a person, I am worthy of chasing accomplishments, and that alone makes me deserving of the opportunity to continue my education.

## 16. LET YOURSELF DOWN LAST

So often, as parents, we put ourselves on the back burner. Our dreams often get forgotten somewhere between the time we are changing diapers and the moment we are celebrating our child's high school graduation. Society tells you to put your children first, always without question.

Yet, I strongly advocate the opposite. Let yourself down last. Fill your bucket so that when your children are fighting for the twelfth hour in a row, or when your school partner doesn't show up to class with their portion of the project done, you have the capacity to show up for them, and ultimately for yourself. There will be moments throughout your school program that someone, maybe even someone you love, will feel frustration or anger that you are choosing you- do it anyway. You are a person, and if being in school is where your heart and passion tells you to be, then show up, yes- even if only for you.

Say those words to yourself as often as you need to, until you begin putting your words into actions: I let myself down last. I am worthy of my dreams.

## 17. BE WHERE YOUR BODY IS

One Monday evening, during a leadership seminar, I was feeling incredibly down about not being present for dinner and bedtime stories. It was the first time I had left my husband with all four of our children, the youngest not yet even three-months old. I spent the first hour clock-watching wondering how dinner was going, if the boys ate, how many ounces our daughter drank and how the new bedtime routine was going. As the rabbithole of wrong turns spun in my mind, I felt my pulse increase and my anxiety become almost unbearable. I was physically sitting in a meeting that I was clearly not ingesting. Not only was I not any help to my husband, I was also not present or contributing to my leadership classmates. Worse, I was texting my husband, desperate to know how things were going. In reality, I was only adding to his anxiety, and making it fairly obvious that I was a mess.

After a few deep breaths and a friendly reminder that tonight they are not my monkeys, and it is not in fact my circus, I refocused and accepted that I was there, in that meeting until 8:00pm. By the time I arrived at home each of our four children would be asleep, my husband would be exhausted, and it would best serve our family if I was a breath of fresh air, rather than a tsunami ready to completely take over our home.

You've made the schedules, you have strong routines, and you understand your why. Now all that is left, is to trust yourself. Trust that you've made the right decision, trust that your support system and children understand that you are taking care of yourself. Be where your body is, not where your mind or socitial or anyone else's guilt may want you to be. If you made the decision to spend the next thirty minutes on your thesis- show up, put your head down and get to work. If you made the decision to skip reading the optional reading for class to take your children out to ice cream- show up, eat the ice cream and enjoy those belly laughs. Be where your body is.

## 18. YOU WILL ENCOUNTER A CURVE BALL- BE FLEXIBLE

A few months into beginning my second graduate degree, I found out I was pregnant. A few weeks later, I miscarried, for the second time. I was devastated. Having one miscarriage was common, something that while we never experienced with our first three children, was statistically a tragedy I could wrap my brain around. Having a second miscarriage, nearly broke me. For months I struggled, mostly in silence. I was going through the motions, but everything around me was seeming to march forward at warp speed. My routines and systems kept me productive and accountable, especially during moments I felt creatively depleted.

Time continued to pass, and a few months later, again, we were pregnant. I spent the majority of those first few weeks holding my breath, terrified of again not having the opportunity to meet our child. A few additional weeks passed, and as my sickness increased, my worry about our baby decreased. As I began to allow myself to plan for our fourth child, I quickly realized that, as far as my graduate program was concerned, the timing of our pregnancy was fairly terrible. I would be giving birth during our internship- the very four weeks that I believed were going to be my favorite. The next month, only a few weeks later, as a class we would then begin an intense two weeks of thesis writing. Fourteen eight or nine hour days, only five weeks after my due date.

Emotionally motivated, I got to work. With the help of an amazing professor, I made a plan to increase my practicum hours and also complete my internship during the spring semester, all before giving birth. With the help of my principal, I completed the intense twenty-two page introductory chapter to my thesis, before the end of the school year and my due date. I also then made the difficult decision to take two weeks of my maternity leave, in the middle of my summer off and precious time with our last child, and spend them with my classmates, working towards my dream of completing my Educational Leadership degree.

I left my six week (she came a week early) old baby in the loving arms of my mother-in-law and for two weeks, I went to class. Having done my written work early, I had the majority of my evenings open to love on our children and attempt to rest for the next day's class. It was intense. It was hard. I do not regret a moment of it.

# 19. BE HONEST ABOUT THE TIME COMMITMENT

Assignments, internships, thesis writing, dedicated research- they all take time. In fact, they take a lot of time. Be honest with yourself, and your loved ones about how much time you'll need to complete the work. Interview individuals who have gone through your program, plan for assignments to take longer than you anticipate. Do not expect people to cover your shifts, or for your spouse to pick up your household responsibilities because you did not manage your time well. Do not convince yourself that you can get a novel and five pages written in three hours. Your inability to access your project accurately will cause unnecessary stress.

## 20. APOLOGIZE WHEN YOU NEED TO

So you screwed up, it happens. Good people screw up, and let's face it- yes, even you will screw up. You will pick your kid up at the wrong time, or miscalculated the amount of time you needed to finish your lab report. You are human, and while you should work to avoid these errors, they are going to happen. Don't let them become a habit, but also don't let them provide you a source of guilt or excuse. Own your mistakes and put in the work to correct them in the future.

One afternoon, incredibly excited, and after telling the kids that morning, I called the school asking the secretary to let their teachers know to head outside after school. A reminder that I was picking them up early. I watched the clock closely, internally calculating the four minute drive to their elementary school added with the three to four minute lag time it most likely would take for boys to gather their belongings, say goodbye to friends and find each other outside of the school's main entrance. I arrived promptly at 3:18pm. Confused by the lack of other cars, or well really the presence of any other cars or students, I was completely baffled by what was going on. I arrived exactly three minutes after the bell, three minutes- while likely enough time for the older boys to make their way outside, was surely not enough time for every other kid in school to get to where they were going. In a slight panic, I parked our van, threw my mask on (thanks, 2020) and rushed towards the school's entrance.

Almost immediately, Maverick, our oldest son, asked me what took so long. Three minutes, I said- I am here three minutes after the bell. Our eyes met, both completely perplexed by the other's confused glare. Still not understanding, I encouraged Maverick to share his feelings. Even as he was talking, it took a few additional minutes before I realized that the school day ends, not at 3:15, but at 3:00 sharp. I was in fact, eighteen minutes, rather than three late. Eighteen minutes between the end of the day and my arrival explained the lack of cars, children, and slightly frustrated children. The anticipation I provided that morning, along with the call to the school left our oldest son petrified for eighteen minutes. While the entire thing was slightly embarrassing, I mean this was his third year at the same school, and a complete misunderstanding, the act warranted an apology. I apologized to my son, owned my actions and together we went on with our special activity.

Of course not every apology worthy act is this minor- yet, the message is still the same. Big or small, apologize when you need to.

## 21. KNOW WHAT NEEDS EXTRA ATTENTION AND WHAT DOESN'T

Let go of the idea that everything you complete will be Pinterest worthy. Not every assignment needs to be first in class, and not every moment with your children needs to be Disney World special. Learn which assignments you need to nail, and which ones are fluff or preparing your for larger projects. Give extra effort where needed, but don't add the pressure of being perfect with every assignment, or during every dinner. You will not have the time or energy to win every award.

During the first summer of my recent course work, my fellow Cadre members and I would, every few days, quietly walk around the room, laptops open displaying one of our most recent assignments- a reflection visual. The visual, alongside a well narrated caption would later on build portfolio entries for our student website detailing our growth as an Educational Leader.

Early on in these tasks, which by the end of our course work, included well over forty assignments, I acknowledged my lack of creativity or desired amount of time wanting to spend on their completion. While I admired my classmates' work, I became okay with not having this be my moment of acceleration. I completed the tasks, including all essential elements, both in checklist and while meeting the requested date of completion. All on time, all meeting requirements, none of which were ever front of the room showing off worthy. Early on I decided this is not where I wanted to spend my time excelling.

There was however, a time, during the first class, the end of our first two weeks of the next two years together, that I decided to show my cards. Working with a new classmate, I took a risk, and advocated that we revamp an Ed Sheeran hit into a remix of review from material presented in class. We worked together to change the lyrics, and with the help of my husband, and several hours of learning new software, perfected a YouTube karaoke version of our Ed Sheeran hit.

Having the karaoke lyrics and video ready to go, and as my heart was pounding out of my chest, I knew this was the moment I could make a lasting first- impression on both my peers and my professors. Giving this everything I had, holding back all anxiety and self- doubt, I took the mic, cranked the volume and asked everyone to stand up and sing along with me as, with the help of an Ed Sheeran hit, we sang along to our class review.

This moment helped define who I would be in our class for the next two years. I took a risk, and for me this played out much better than the less than astounding work I had completed for my reflections.

## 22. YOU WILL SNAP

At some point, you'll totally lose it. Assignments will pile up, someone at work will not do their part, and each of your children, potentially even your spouse will be angry with you. Everything will feel hard, and without any warning, you will snap. Even well prepared and planned people miscalculate or misplace things from time to time. Work to lessen these blows, and provide yourself grace when you need.

## 23. DON'T SIGN YOURSELF UP FOR EXTRAS

At your staff meeting, when everyone is signing up for an extra volunteer basketball to cover, or when your professor needs someone to come in early and help organize papers, do not sign up. You, a full-time working parent, who is now also in school, is already doing extra. Do not give into the pressure to do more, especially more than you actually want to do, or know is reasonably achievable. Show up for what you've already signed up for, knock your current obligations out of the park, and save the extras for people who have extra time. Then one day, in the future, when your life calms down, it will be your turn to pay it forward.

## 24. SAVE THE EXCUSES

Many times throughout my career, or within adult friendships, people have disclosed that they didn't extend an invitation, or ask for my time because they knew I had a family at home. Assuming that I wouldn't be able to go, or wondering if I would make the time, even if well intended were hurtful assumptions that, at times, provided missed opportunities for growth. While I may not always be able to say yes, I always want to be extended the chance, if I am in fact able to provide advancement or worth to the event or conversation.

I want to be taken seriously, with or without children. I do not want others to use my children as an excuse, and therefore, I also do not get to use them as an excuse. Do not use your children or your school obligations as an excuse. Everyone is busy, yes- even young Sally who is not married, or does not have any children. Her time is just as important as yours, and while it may be easy to blame the kids for your inability to meet to complete your group project- do not place blame. Figure out a way to complete your commitments. No one will trust or respect you if you fill your portion with excuses or wish I coulds.

## 25. ACT IN YOUR VALUES

Reflect and actually know the beliefs that drive you forward. Understand the person you are and the things that are important to you. Then simply put- live only in a way that demonstrates your beliefs. Complete your assignments and participate in family time that only ring true to your character. Surround yourself with positive affirmations and create the environment that moves you forward. Temptation will find you, forgetting assignments, not showing up for a team member, all of these things may become attractive to you as you push through your degree. Do not let your busy schedule change who you are, or how you treat people.

## 26. COMPLETE TASKS IN CHUNKS

Many times with a lot of items on your list, you'll need to utilize your time and resources wisely. When miracles happen and your kids are occupied, or they sleep in an extra hour, use the time to knock out your must do tasks. Thirty minutes here and there add up. If your life is like mine, it is highly unlikely that with children you'll have multiple hours set aside, especially in the evenings or weekends to do things without interruption. Complete routine or mindless tasks in ten- or fifteen minute intervals, breaking larger tasks into smaller manageable items. Save the really intricate responsibilities for the time you've scheduled.

I was always amazed at the things I could accomplish if I spent the extra ten to twenty minutes here and there being productive rather than browsing through Facebook. An email to arrange internship hours, scheduling a meeting, responding to a parent inquiry, or making an online grocery order- all things that independently are not time consuming or difficult- yet, together, at once, can take up a lot of time and mental energy. Taking advantage of small chunks of time allowed me to really dive into tasks or assignments that required a lot of new thinking and project development during the infrequent isolated work time that I had.

## 27. SELF-CARE WILL LOOK DIFFERENT

While I don't expect that as a person, you should lose yourself, I also think it's important for you to understand that weekly trips to the spa are likely a thing of the past, or at least not a part of your current reality. While taking care of yourself used to look like all-day Netflix binge watching, or girls night every Wednesday, it is very probable that the way you will take care of yourself is different. Self-care, of course, while more difficult to achieve, is incredibly important and still can be realistic. Take care of yourself, but figure out a way to do this in ways that work with your current schedule, rather than long, unrealistic benders.

## 28. YOU WILL BE EXHAUSTED

Attempting to be super-human, also known as chasing your dreams, while not impossible, will leave you completely exhausted. Every week after working, turning in assignments, and parenting our four children, I'd collapse on the couch completely asleep, unable to move by 7:00pm. While many of the tasks I was completing day after day were enjoyable, constantly being on full-steam ahead mode caught up to me. Even if in the best way, I was exhausted. Give yourself permission to leave the lists for another time, and do exactly what your body needs it to do- rest.

## 29. FIND SUPPORT- YOU'LL NEED IT

We've all heard the over used phrase It takes a village, yet what people often leave out is the difficulty of establishing these friendships, or systematic support groups. With intention, figure it out, work to develop support in each of the aspects of what you are attempting to accomplish. Find people who support your career, your schooling, and your children. These people do not have to be your friends, or your family- sometimes the best support comes from a paid babysitter, the house cleaner, or the custodian (thank you, Teresa) at your school. Find your people, lean on and learn from them- you will need the support.

## 30. LOOK AHEAD

If you're not planning ahead, you're already behind. Having a buffet sized appetite on your toddler size plate is nearly impossible to conquer, without a plan. If you have an extra month in the summer without classes, or a week when you're not working, or that magical one day a year when you don't work but your kids are in school- plan ahead and use these precious hours wisely. Use your time and energy well. Think about what you can do now, without creating extra stress, that can help you later? Extra practicum hours? Read the novel? A much needed pedicure? Whatever you need to do, look ahead- use your time.

## 31. EVALUATE YOUR ROUTINE

The system you set up at the beginning of the semester, or even the one you tried to introduce last week- take the time to assess its effectiveness. If your routine isn't working, adjust it. Routines are rituals that legendary people create, and while most successful people have them, they do not look the same. I'd venture to assume that their systems continue to change, as they grow or their tasks change. Be flexible, figure out what works and what doesn't. If it doesn't- no shame, try something new. Failure doesn't come from trying, it comes from not changing- not moving forward.

## 32. SURROUND YOURSELF WITH PEOPLE WHO SUPPORT YOU

Your long time friend who doesn't understand your career, family or school choice, is not the person you need to spend your precious time with. Outside of an individual being genuinely curious and wanting to support your endeavours, do not accept or allow negativity to enter your life. You have no time, or room for people who want to judge your or make small dabs at your decisions. Stay strong in your decision, and find people who lift you up, instead of bring you down.

## 33. TAKE YOURSELF AND YOUR GOALS SERIOUSLY

In attempts of not wanting to make someone else feel bad, or to appear as though I put myself on a pedestal, I would often downplay the work and effort I was completing every day. Instead of being proud of my accomplishments, and speaking openly about them, I would make myself and my accomplishments appear smaller than they actually were. I was minimizing my efforts to make everyone else feel better.

During my graduate school intake interview, my soon-to-be professor directly proclaimed that the program I had applied for required a lot of time, and serious dedication. Not tip toeing, she explained that completing this program with three small children would be a difficult task. Without flinching, and while hiding my annoyance, I used this moment as an opportunity to lay all of my cards out on the table. Looking her straight in the eye, I- without hesitation, passionately demonstrated my ability to successfully complete the program.

Take yourself seriously, especially if you expect anyone else to.

## 34. DO NOT WAIT FOR AN OPPORTUNITY

Job shadows, internships and practicum hours are likely going to be required prior to the completion of your degree. Do not wait for an opportunity to come to you. Be proactive, make inquiries and be selective. If you are going to be spending time away from your career and your family, ensure that you are spending your time with an organization and people who are worth your time. Provide yourself enough time to do proper research not only having completed a checkbox for your program, but a potential advocate for your future. Ensure that the opportunity works with your schedule, rather than running around last minute trying to find extra daycare or leaving your significant other with one more day alone with the kids. Make things happen, do not wait for things to hopefully, or maybe fall into your lap.

During both years of my graduate program, I found myself in a situation where I needed to spend multiple days shadowing a school administrator. Different leadership opportunities came with different requirements. Assignment expectations that were time intensive. With intentional planning, and not wanting to use much, if any, of my personal leave, I researched nearby school districts that had different Spring Breaks than my district, or which schools were in session on Martin Luther King Day, when our district gave it to us off. Thinking through these situations, being creative and advocating for these opportunities allowed for me to complete these tasks without additional stress.

## 35. USE YOUR PTO WHEN YOU NEED TO

Most of my paid days off were used tending to sick kids. Yet, when used wisely, and sparingly, I provided myself with enough paid time off to take a full day, at home- in silence, to complete the final chapter and proofreading needed to submit all one hundred and twenty-two pages of thesis to my professor. I needed a full day to get to the finish line, not wanting to use an entire weekend day away from my family, I decided using my PTO was my best option. Alone, at home, I was able to buckle down and complete the assignment in one day, and two weeks before the assignment was due. Find ways to make potentially stressful moments less stressful. Do not work harder than you need to. Work to dimminse stress, rather than hoping it all just works out.

## 36. SET MINI-MILESTONES

Celebratory milestones are not limited to the end of a semester, or program. High-five yourself, intentionally recognizing that you showed up for yourself and that you are putting in the work. Set mini-milestones that credit the work and sacrifice that you are displaying. Give yourself permission to whoo-hoo each difficult task. You are worth it.

## 37. LET YOUR FAMILY SEE YOU SUCCEED

Do your school work in front of your family, talk about how you overcame a challenging assignment, discuss the times you had the courage to openly engage in a difficult conversation with a peer. Provide opportunities for your children to catch your work ethnic and courage.

My graduate graduation day was not as we expected thanks to the necessary COVID-19 quarantine regulations. Yet, when May 9, 2020, my conventional graduation Saturday, my husband insisted that on the day I was scheduled to walk the stage and receive my diploma, that we, as a family, would still acknowledge my accomplishment. That morning, he set up a tripod, focused the camera, got all four of our small children dressed, and ensured that we got a family photo with mom in her graduation cap and gown. The act of having our children see me in my graduation regalia was important, not just to me, but for my husband as well.

Be intentional with what you show your children. So much of what they learn will forever be caught rather than taught. Let your family share and learn from your success.

## 38. TREAT YOURSELF

Yes, the "Parks and Rec" saying lives on to see another day, and while it may now be ten years old, the simple phrase is still true today. Treat-yo-self. Treat yourself to ice cream, an extra run, an hour in the sunshine, treat yourself to a night out with your friends, or an extra game of Skip Bo with your children. Whatever it is that you do to recognize that you are in fact doing it, do that- with intention, without apology.

## 39. INTENTIONALLY FIND JOY

There will be moments, maybe even full semesters where you will wonder why you signed yourself up for this. You will contemplate your sanity and begin wondering if all of the work is really worth it. Find the joy. Make a list of your why, reflect on your growth, practice gratitude and dig as deep as you need to to fill up your bucket. You signed up for this program because continuing your education lit a fire inside you. Find your joy and use it to push you forward.

## 40. SOMEONE WILL GET SICK

It is inevitable, your children will get sick. You will have to miss, reschedule or juggle an important work event, class or job shadowing opportunity. When there is a meeting you cannot miss, or an assignment that cannot be late, have a plan to both show up for your family and your goals. And, of course, when the unexpected truly happens, be where you need to be. During my second year in my Educational Leadership program, only three days after teacher's reported back to our classrooms, we discovered that my daughter had a pyloric stenosis requiring an immediate surgery and three day hospital stay. My graduate work took the back burner, as did my classroom obligations. I needed to be with my family. Your children will get sick, you will likely miss something important, don't let the fear of the struggle keep you from trying. You will figure it out, everything will be okay.

# 41. GIVE YOURSELF FAMILY DUE DATES

Your course work, and likely even your job will come with strict deadlines. You will have more due-dates than you'd likely like to shuffle, and while it may be easiest to prioritize these responsibilities, be mindful not to allow your family to take the back burner. Your school will come with deadlines, make sure your family time does as well. Do not allow yourself to go six months between dates with your spouse. Do not forgo family obligations that provide them and yourself with joy. Your family will never give you a due-date, they will never place a timestamp on how long they'll wait for your undivided attention. Do not take advantage of their support. Schedule time with family members if you need to- give yourself a deadline to make them feel your love. Show them how much you appreciate their support.

## 42. YOU DON'T KNOW WHAT YOU DON'T KNOW

Give yourself a little grace. To be fair, you really have no idea what you're signing yourself up for, how challenging or time consuming going back to school will really be until of course your knee deep into your program. You simply don't know, what you don't know. Of course, once you do know- do better. When something is not working out, figure out another way. Your dedication to your family and your career don't have to ruin relationships or break you down. Do your best with the information you're given, and have enough faith in yourself that when your system isn't working, you'll find a new solution.

# 43. YOU DECIDE YOUR TIMELINE

Most programs, traditional or non, will have wiggle room in the amount of time from beginning to end. My most recent degree was built with the intention of each student belonging to a no more than thirty-five group member cadre. In design all cadre members begin and end their program together. Each cadre member takes the same classes, at the same time, only having their practicum, internship and thesis vary.

Finding myself pregnant, and with our due date being during a critical point in our program I had a choice- get creative in how I complete my internship prior to having our fourth child, and then return to class less than a month after giving birth, or do I pause, join a different group and graduate a year later. I made the decision to stick with my cadre. I decided my timeline. Your program will stretch over several years, if it feels right to slow things down, do so. Do what works for you and your family, going slower than others, or taking a break does not discredit your dedication to your education. Many of my group members added endorsements or started their doctorate right after our graduation, that timeline doesn't work for my family. I did the barebones, I fulfilled my graduation requirements- nothing less, and nothing more.

## 44. YOU MIGHT CHANGE YOUR MIND

You likely have a beautiful mental image of your graduation day. Mentally you've selected the dress you'll wear, the thank you notes you'll write and the celebratory cake you'll buy. You may have mentally given yourself career expectations that accompany this new found education, and well- then reality may come and you just might not want to do any of that. You are a constantly evolving human, and if like mine, the program you are embarking on is likely to change your life, yes- even if it does so in ways you could have never expected. Wanting to graduate with my leadership degree, with in fact, a new administrative leadership title, I worked day and night, for over eighteen months. While we were not supposed to admit to ourselves, or others, that this was our objective, I mentally had my next five years strategically planned out. Life happened, and after my daughter was hospitalized for the second time in her six months of life, and with and an additional human life, one I didn't even know I'd have when I started my graduate program, my career aspirations dramatically shifted. I changed my mind. My goals changed, the outcome of the way I'd use my degree changed. My work ethic, my passion and my desire to finish strong did not change, yet- most everything else certainly had. I changed, and it turns out- I'm now even better.

I am a better person because I pursued and finished my graduate program.

## 45. MANTRAS AND AFFIRMATIONS

Find positivity and surround yourself with them. Write a mantra, record an affirmation, do whatever it is so that you can push yourself to accomplish your goals. My professor, early on into our course work encouraged us, in passing, to make our email password, a simple mantra. Something that you'd be forced to type and mentally recite every single time you logged into your computer or email. I took her advice, and several times a day I used this simple task as a way to remember my values and the goals I was reaching towards.

Surround yourself with people and places that lift you up, and challenge you to be better. If that environment or those people do not exist for you, push forward- create your atmosphere and look for new people.

# 46. TALK WITH YOUR FAMILY MEMBERS

Do not assume that your children will not be influenced by your decision to go back to school. Talk with your kids about their feelings, any frustrations they had during your last semester, or how they'd like your time together to look. Maybe they'd love to have you as a study partner at the library for a few hours on Sunday. Maybe your spouse really needs to sit down for a Friday night movie to feel as though you're still there for them. Allow your family members to be a part of the conversation that helps move you forward in your goals.

Through my recent schooling, as well as through many of the seemingly adult tasks I complete on a daily basis, I intentionally attempt to engage our children into a conversation about my actions. I read books in front of them to show, rather than just tell them that reading is the gateway to success and gaining knowledge. I openly talk about career goals, or when to take more time for family. I ask questions and am curious about their interpretation to what I am doing behind my computer screen on the weekends. I explain why I am home late or gone all day for class. Opening dialogue, understanding that the journey to conquering your dreams stretches far beyond yourself.

## 47. SELECT YOUR NON NEGOTIABLES

In delicate attempts to juggle a large amount of obligations, give yourself permission to decide what events are important, how your time is spent, and how you'll be treated by others. Making these decisions allows your responsibilities to influence the mental health of each of your family members (including yourself). Select, on purpose, what is not negotiable for you. Your time, and potentially your patience will be thin, recognizing your non negotiables allows for you to without hesitation spend your time appropriately.

## 48. YOU WILL FEEL OVERWHELMED

Outside of being exhausted, you will also be overwhelmed. Without a doubt, you will be presented with a situation in which you did not plan for, nor do you know how to proceed. Multiple commitments will need your attention, your system will have failed and most likely someone will feel as though you dropped the ball. You are capable of completing your school requirements, but having this capacity does not void you from being human.

Attempting to expect the unexpected, all while planning for what you already know to expect, is thoroughly debilitating. Juggling a career, school and your family is challenging enough, even more so when the objects your juggling change without warning. The system you created was lost, the training you spent hours revamping went another direction, your husband needs to work late leaving you to pick up all of the children, or your fourth kid tested positive for Influenza B, leaving this the 21st straight day that someone in your immediate family has had a temperature.

Acknowledging that you will be overwhelmed allows you to have the courage to step back, practice self-care and evaluate your immediate needs. Stay calm and stay in it- you can get through this moment.

## 49. JUST SHOW UP

Sometimes the hardest, yet greatest accomplishment is the simple act of showing up. Time and time again, even against all the odds put up against you, you just need to simply show up. When you aren't sure of how you'll get an assignment done. If you don't know if your daughter wants you at her basketball game, or if Susie, the student-friend, needs your assistance making final touches to your group project. Just show up. Be someone people can count on, be a person you can count on. Show up, stay in it and slowly you'll figure it out.

## 50. YOU CAN DO HARD THINGS

Raise your right hand and repeat after me: My name is (fill in the blank) and I can do hard things. Say this to yourself over and over. Say this to yourself so often that you, and maybe even the people around you can anticipate the inspiring words that are about to leave your mouth. Your thoughts determine your actions, and your actions become your accomplishments. You are capable of greatness, you can achieve your goals. You can get through hard moments. You are (fill in the blank) and you do hard things.

# READ OTHER 50 THINGS TO KNOW BOOKS

50 Things to Know to Get Things Done Fast: Easy Tips for Success

50 Things to Know About Going Green: Simple Changes to Start Today

50 Things to Know to Live a Happy Life Series

50 Things to Know to Organize Your Life: A Quick Start Guide to Declutter, Organize, and Live Simply

50 Things to Know About Being a Minimalist: Downsize, Organize, and Live Your Life

50 Things to Know About Speed Cleaning: How to Tidy Your Home in Minutes

50 Things to Know About Choosing the Right Path in Life

50 Things to Know to Get Rid of Clutter in Your Life: Evaluate, Purge, and Enjoy Living

50 Things to Know About Journal Writing: Exploring Your Innermost Thoughts & Feelings

# 50 Things to Know

**Stay up to date with new releases on Amazon:**

https://amzn.to/2VPNGr7

# 50 Things to Know

We'd love to hear what you think about our content! Please leave your honest review of this book on Amazon and Goodreads. We appreciate your positive and constructive feedback. Thank you.

Made in United States
Orlando, FL
17 December 2021

11996697R00046